MOM'S POETRY

MOM'S POETRY

KATHLEEN DUNLEAVY

Copyright © 2020 by Kathleen Dunleavy.

ISBN-13: 9781645504559

All rights reserved. No part of this book may be reproduced or transmitted in any form or by any means, electronic or mechanical, including photocopying, recording, or by any information storage and retrieval system, without permission in writing from the copyright owner.

Any people depicted in stock imagery provided by Thinkstock are models, and such images are being used for illustrative purposes only.
Certain stock imagery © Thinkstock.

Artwork by Dr. Frank Stringfellow

CONTENTS

Introduction ix

Childbirth 1
9/11 3
Our Dad 7
Forgiveness 9
An Arduous Journey 11
Loneliness 15
The True Friend 17
Thanksgiving 1998 25
Thanksgiving 2001 27
Thanksgiving 2002 31
Thanksgiving 2004 35
Thanksgiving 2005 39
Thanksgiving 2007 41
Thanksgiving 2008 45
Thanksgiving 2011 49
Thanksgiving 2012 53
Thanksgiving 2013 57
Thanksgiving 2014 61
Thanksgiving 2015 65
Thanksgiving 2016 69
Thanksgiving 2017 73
Thanksgiving 2018 77
Thanksgiving 2019 81

DEDICATION

This book of poetry is dedicated to my wonderful, beloved children Mike, Kate, Mary and Martin and to their beautiful offspring.

INTRODUCTION

In 1998, in preparation for Thanksgiving dinner, Kathleen Dunleavy, matriarch of an enlarging family, decided to write a poem as rhe family's Thanksgiving prayer-before-dinner. There would be a verse for each family member. What began as eight verses in 1998 has grown to twenty-seven verses in 2019 (with couples coupled).

Most verses are descriptive of achievements, one to two each year are devoted to the family's Dad who died in 1995, and some are humorous or divulge a family secret.

In addition to the collection of Thanksgiving Prayer-Poems, Kathleen wrote a powerful poem on 9/11 after guiding her staff at New York-Presbyterian Hospital, where she was a Patient Care Director until her retirement in 2011, in preparing Intensive Care Unit beds for the victims of the horrible holocaust.

More and more poems have been written on primarily solemn subjects and complete "Mom's Poetry", designed to give her children and grandchildren remembrances found in one central location.

In addition to her book of poetry, Kathleen has published clinical journal articles and two clinical textbook chapters.

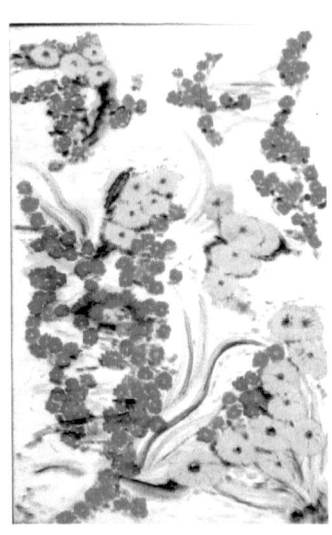

Flowers in Front of the Lawyer's Office. (2/2002). Oil and acrylic on canvas. 24x36 inches. On 9/11/01 terrorists attacked the twin towers in the U.S. I did pastels of flowers during the following ten days. I've never done pastels in my life. It's funny how such beauty could come from such tragedy. I wrote poetry instead.

Bee Balm 1 (Looking Down) (7-9-/2010) Acrylic on canvas. 30x34 inches. Bee Balm is a common wild flower east of the Mississippi.

CHILDBIRTH

At the start of every labor
A deepening peace sets in
A feeling of expectance
Something sacred to begin

A feeling of a miracle
About to manifest
God hovering very closely
To assure this child is blessed

The feeling is of moving
Into a deep and sacred place
And only do I awaken
When this baby meets my gaze

F-15 E Over the Appalachians or Sept. 12. On Station over the Appalachians. (2/2002). Acrylic on hardboard. 16x20 inches. I saw these planes go up to put a blanket over the Washington Baltimore area after Sept. 11. I saw a F-18 Hornet with after-burners blazing going north to Pennsylvania to intercept the plane that was lost that day over Pennsylvania.

9/11

Our freedom is shattered
Our country's at war
Our people are shaken
Right through to their core

The towers have fallen
So hard to believe
Destruction and death
Behind it did leave

Where did this come from
This horror so real
How could such a nightmare
Have struck us so near

Why did this happen
This carnage occur
How bless-ed our landscape
How peaceful we were

Incredible suffering
No end to the pain
It's doubtful that ever
Our heartache will wane

Tragedy reigning
The death toll so high
The embers still rising
As far as the sky

Trying to find
Anyone we can save
No end to the rosters
Of helpers so brave

Will we ever recover
Know peace once again
Or does this awful happening
Signal an end

We've all come together
Created a bond
Our flags we are flying
Our uniforms donned

We ask for assistance
From heaven above
To help ease the burden
To bring back the doves

We pray for our friends
Who were struck down so hard
May they be eased from
The pain in their hearts

We thank you for leaving
Our family intact
Our help and assistance
We gladly give back

God bless our great Country
May peace come again
At best may we ask that
This holocaust end

God bless America
Ever so free
And God bless our planet
Of land and of sea

May all of us savor
Each day and each hour
May love for each other
Be our comfort and power

By Kathleen Dunleavy
Columbia Presbyterian Medical Center
17 September 2001

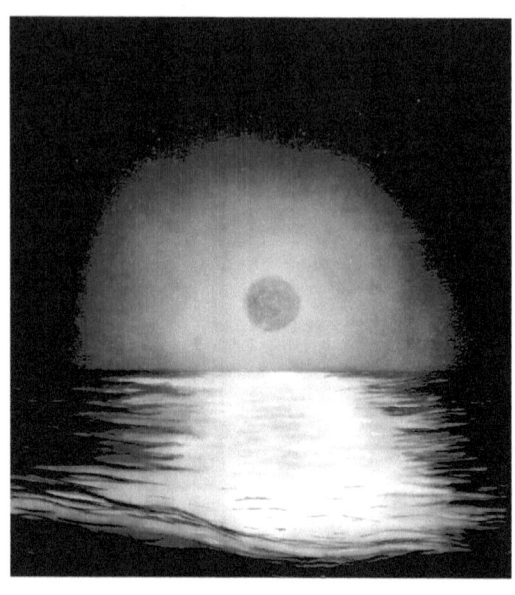

Moon Doggy (Moon Rising off Cobb Island.) (6/16/2009). Acrylic and air brush on canvas. 38 x 39 inches. Cobb island is a barrier island in the Atlantic. It makes you seem so small as you stand on the beach in the moonlight. The moon just hangs in space. A full moon this low on the horizon has an orange color as a result of atmospheric distortion and it appears bigger than it really is. I call it Moon Doggy. I attribute this latter effect to lensing because there is more atmosphere that the light has to go through.

OUR DAD

Our Dad has peacefully left us
Martin checked him and found him still
It was totally unexpected
But obviously was God's will

He never saw a wedding
And missed so much of our lives
He only met one grandchild
And didn't see everyone thrive

Although he left us too early
Many a gift he left behind
He taught us all to savor
The gift of the human mind

He deeply loved his children
And nurtured them in powerful ways
He showed them the path to follow
To succeed for all their days

We thank our God for Dad's lifetime
And for all he deemed to give
To our very grateful family
Who wishes he still lived

Dad is still always with us
Only in a different way
He watches us and prays
For our welfare every day

*Stream at East Entrance of Greenbelt Park. (1/24/2004).
Acrylic on canvas. 20 x 24 inches.*

FORGIVENESS

"Bless me, Father, for I have sinned"
Is music to God's ears
And our pastoral provider
Is there to calm our fears

God does not expect perfection
He knows we all have flaws
None of us are perfect
We all have taken falls

God is merciful and loving
He wants us by His side
He accepts our every downfall
And gives us back our pride

When we honestly repent
And ask for God's forgiveness
He rejoices at our honesty
And celebrates our goodness

Blarney Castle in Moonlight (10/2015). Acrylic and airbrush on canvas. 36x48 inches. The second that I saw this perspective I knew how I was going to do this painting. I imagined it and made it happen.

AN ARDUOUS JOURNEY

I once believed
But then I didn't
And life was not as good

I could not understand
My crumbling life
And my thoughts didn't feel as they should

I stumbled along
Down my tortuous path
Seeking many kinds of solace

I feared all the while
For my treasured children
That their scars could turn to malice

My dream of being
The perfect Mother
Was slowly fading away

And even my therapist
Whom I saw forever
Couldn't help me find my way

Then one day in the kitchen
Four children looked at me
I couldn't drive to soccer and no dinner was in sight

That day, for the very first time
I had a drink in the morning
I knew the battle was over and alcohol had won the fight

I went to Detox and Rehab
And dreaded returning to work
Professionally, I was mortified and ashamed

But AA's support was significant
I was an officer within a year
And I began to look at the strengths I'd attained

Many years went by
And things were hard but better
And then I knew what was missing

The only hope for finding peace
And overcoming the emptiness
Almost certainly was believing

I tried on my own
To regain my faith
But my efforts came up bare

Without any help
I just trodded on
And lamented my failure to get there

Then a rainbow appeared
In the form of a friend
An old friend from a distant land

As his faith and holiness
Supported and helped me
My hands finally found God's hands

Was it a miracle?
Was it the seeking of help?
Maybe even a stroke of good luck for me?

Only God, Who was always watching
Knows the answer to this query
How blessed I am in accepting the love plan from Thee

The children they have thrived
The four have ten degrees
And they have blessed me with eleven offspring

I retired in good standing
With awards and recognitions
I was honored but mostly blessings did these bring

I have a holy Friend
To go to and cry
And I trust His plan for me

I'm no longer alone
Someone is watching
How blessed could I be?

*Kootenay National Park. (9/2016). Woodburning.
Kootenay National Park is in Alberta, Canada.*

Lantern (Haunting) (8/18/2009). Airbrush, acrylic and oil on board. 9 x 12 inches. My son John and I went to the Monitor Center at the Maritime Museum in Newport News. This lamp was the lead-in exhibit. I had to paint it and bring it home. It is the lamp that they last saw of the Monitor as it sank in the storm. My wife Therese called the painting haunting.

LONELINESS

Loneliness is not alone
Loneliness is alone in pain

Loneliness is an empty space
Aloneness can be a *fulfilling* space

Loneliness is filled with sadness
Aloneness can help you *cope* with sadness

Loneliness does not see hope
Aloneness sometimes *dreams* of hope

Loneliness suggests a need
Aloneness can be what *fills* a need

Loneliness usually needs relief
Aloneness sometimes *brings* relief

Loneliness is not relieved from within
Loneliness needs our help from *without*

Sonny and Buster. (9/10/2014). Acrylic and oil canvas. 16 x 20 inches. True friends! Dogs give unconditional love.

THE TRUE FRIEND

In times of needed secrecy
The true friend doesn't tell

In times of needed advisement
The true friend gives his all

In times of confessing
The true friend does not betray

In times of trouble
The true friend listens

In times of self-doubt
The true friend supports

In times of sadness
The true friend grieves

In times of loss
The true friend is there

In times of success
The true friend is joyful

In times of loneliness
The true friend comes or calls

In times of discouragement
The true friend supports

In times of failure
The true friend understands

In times of anger
The true friend calms

In times of fear
The true friend comforts

In Loving Memory of
Patricia A. Molden

Our beautiful Patty has left us
She's now in the arms of God's love
She leaves behind a lifetime of giving
Now she's our Heart, Strength, and Angel Dove

Her thoughts were always of others
She loved to see everyone pleased
Her words of others were kind ones
Her favors never ceased

She deeply loved her grandsons
Her daughter and her son
She provided a home for her Mom and Dad
In their last years in the sun

Thank you, God, for giving us Patty
And for her endurance that never ceased
And thank you, Patty, for all you've shown us
About giving and loving and peace

In Loving Memory of
Mary C. Doman

Mary was called to heaven
Her last few years were hard
Her reward, of course, was waiting
She is now in the arms of Our Lord

Mary adored her children
And loved her grandchildren as well
She was always so proud of her family
Many tales of them she would tell

She was always filled with beauty
From her birth through every day
And her beauty was filled with sweetness
As though an angel she portrayed

Mary's spirituality was strong
She worshipped God and the Virgin Mother
She set a beautiful example
To her family and many others

Thank you, God, for giving us Mary
And for her kindness every day
And thank you, Mary, for loving us
In your very special way

The Horn of Plenty. (In Celebration of Fall). (6/2010).
Acrylic and oil on canvas. 46 x 75 inches.
This painting was laborious to do because each element required attention to detail. Particularly the fruits and vegetables because each one had to be done right and recognizable in its own right. The first element was the sky, the second the field, third the barn and the tractor with the driver. The field was up at Thurmont, MD. Therese and I were driving home and we saw this scene and I knew that it was ideal for this painting.
The barn was over at Lewes, DEL.
The fruits and vegetables came from the farmers market in Greenbelt and the herbarium at Niagara Falls, NY.
The leaves unify the cornucopia with the fall mountain scene. The oak leaf provides a break to the open field and gives dimension to it. The basket with corn indicates the presence of man without spelling it out since someone had to be there to pack it. The twin boom cornucopia balances out the two silos. A single boom cornucopia was just too boring to me.

THANKSGIVING 1998

We thank you for Mary's passing the Bar
She's a very smart cookie and will surely go far

We thank you for Martin's Law SAT score
And pray that success will come more and more

We thank you for Katy's and Kurt's fruitful jobs
And may their house soon be filled with a mob

For Catrin and Mike a lovely new home
To fill with three beautiful children's tones

We thank you for Marcie's being here
And rejoice in her coming to live so near

For Kellie and Christian – a wonderful pair
Who bring us their happiness here to share

We know that Pop wishes that he were here
But always we know that his presence is near

Most of all we have all gathered here
To give you our thanks for a bless-ed year

AMEN

THANKSGIVING 2001

We're here once again
To thank You and pray
It's been a hard year
There's so much to say

Our footing was shaken
Our security lost
A holocaust came
Many lives it did cost

You spared us much pain
We hardly were touched
For this we were thankful
Through all that we watched

We pray for all victims
For lives torn apart
Our hearts are with them
As they make a new start

For us, we are grateful
For the year we have had
All things considered
It wasn't so bad

Mike headed West
In a very brave move
Their home is a dream
Their kids in a groove

Katy and Kurt
Now live in Short Hills
And Jack is a joy
As their lives he does fill

Mary changed jobs
Her courage we laud
Her apartment looks great
As Dan sawed and he sawed

Martin is now
In his third and last year
He'll, of course, pass the Bar
Of that we don't fear

Grandma has seen
Her job expand
More work to do
I need more hands

Pop, of course,
Is part of our prayers
He sees from above He's
always there

Thank you again
For blessings and gifts
Our year was fruitful
You gave us some lifts

Another Thanksgiving
Another year
Keep us healthy and well
Keep us free of fear

Amen

THANKSGIVING 2002

We're here once again, Lord
To sing out Your praise
You've guided and helped us
Through all this year's days

My year has been peaceful
Calamity-free
I thank you for giving
This blessing to me

Catrin and Mike are
In the same place
Prosperity kept them
From finding a new base

Megan is growing
At such a quick pace
We're seeing such beauty
Alive in her face

Mikey keeps sprouting
And learning new things
He's thoughtful and caring
And happiness brings

Joey is clever
And, oh, so smart
His happy demeanor
Brings joy to your heart

Katy and Kurt
And children make four
They're gracious and giving
And open their door

Jack is a challenge
And shock you he might
His antics are funny
From morning to night

Annie's a beauty
And also now walks
She's starting to like us
And learning to talk

The days have been happy
For Mary and Fred
It won't be much longer
Until they are wed

Martin is blazing
His way to the sky
He keeps working and working
And never asks why

Today hear our prayers, Lord
We're thankful and glad
The year has been bless-ed
Except we miss Dad

Pop isn't missing
A thing from up high
He guides us and loves us
From his place in the sky

Amen

THANKSGIVING 2004

Our Thanksgiving prayer
Is always the same
Our gratitude's endless
For we know whence it came

Our year's been a good one
We're all here and well
Our lives have been full
With so much to tell

We bought a new shore house
For all to share
It's going to be awesome
To have us all there

Mike continues
To be a success
And Catrin is awesome
We all must confess

Megan's a beauty
And does well in school
She has many talents
She's ever so cool

Mikey is growing
And does well in sports
He's funny and clever
And likes tricks of all sorts

Joey's a wizard
He's smart as a whip
He played cards with Grandma
In the car on a trip

Mary and Fred
Have tied the big knot
They're happy and healthy
And still are besot

Katy has managed
To do many things
She's working and studying
And yet still fun she brings

Kurt, thank God
Is a jack-of-all-trades
He'll tackle most anything
He's never afraid

Jack is in pre-school
And bright as can be
He likes to make friends
Of anyone he sees

Annie's a doll baby
Cute as can be
She's happy and lovey
And such a sweet-pea

Martin's a bachelor
Still free as can be
He wears his success well
His future? We'll see

Mom was surprised
By a major award
And now with the shore house
She seldom is bored

Pop always watches
Over all of us here
He'll always support us
Through all of our fears

Thank you again for a
Bless-ed year past
We all say a prayer
That all this will last

Amen

Prince Edward Hotel at Waterton Lake (Chalet). (2/5/2017) Woodburning. 24 x 48 inches. This is a very impressionistic view of the Chalet at Waterton Lake which is a part of Glacier National Park.

THANKSGIVING 2005

It's that time again
It's Thanksgiving Day
We hope that You'll listen
To us as we pray

We number fourteen now
We're a still-growing clan
We've had many blessings
You've shown us Your hand

The year has been peaceful
We've all got our health
There's much to say thanks for
Your gifts are our wealth

Catrin as always
Prepared our whole feast
The food is delicious
To say the least

Mike is our host again
Gracious and kind
He makes us all comfortable
Time after time

We're so proud of Megan
Our favorite cheerleader
Her talents are many
Not many can beat her

Mikey is becoming
A real handsome guy
He's also courageous
There's not much he won't try

Joey's our wizard
He's agile and smart
He seems to be able
To succeed in all he starts

Martin now owns
His own private place
And at work he was
Also given more space

Grandma continues
Her nursing career
Her time for retirement
Is still not near

Pop as always
Is with us here
We know that he loves us
And holds us dear

Thank you once more
For all we've been given
We know that these things
Are all gifts from heaven

Amen

THANKSGIVING 2007

It's that time
Of year once again
Time to gather
Family and friends

Another good year
We've really been blessed
We gather again
As Thanksgiving guests

Mike and Catrin
Are hosting again
Everything's ready
The meal has begun

Megan is lovely
A beautiful girl
Who's the lucky boy
That gets to give her a whirl

Mikey's becoming
A good-looking guy
I hope that someday he gives
Law School a try

Joey as always
Shines like a star
We know that he'll always
Keep going far

Kate and Kurt
And children make five
Their house is always
Fully alive

Jack is now
A really good reader
His interests all keep him
Busy as a beaver

Annie is now an Irish dancer
And also does gymnastics
It sometimes seems
As though she's elastic

Michael Bjorn
What a guy!
He's cute as a button
Without even a try

Mary and Fred are
Not with us this year
But next year they'll bring
A new little dear

Martin was married
With a magnificent feast
Lauren is beautiful
To say the least

Pop as always
Is hovering near
He watches over us
We needn't fear

Thank you again
For all that You do
To keep us healthy
And happy, too

Amen

THANKSGIVING 2008

We've gathered together
To give You our thanks
With its blessings and gifts
This year really ranks

Mike and Catrin
The perennial hosts
To them and their family
We offer a toast

Megan can drive now
She's past Sweet Sixteen
She's pretty and smart enough
To be a Homecoming Queen

Mikey is growing
Into a fine boy
He just needs to know
That fire's not a toy

Joey has learned
To play the guitar
Who knows but one day
He'll be a big star

Mary is nothing
Short of amazing
As a chef and a lawyer
She keeps her trails blazing

Fred is forever
The perfect father
He's thoughtful and nothing
Is ever a bother

Helena is growing
And now goes to school
She's learning to follow
All of the rules

Margot's our youngest
A cute little thing
She smiles and smiles
And joy does she bring

This is Lauren's
First year here
It's great to have
Her beauty and cheer

Martin has bought
A new house this year
He's climbing the ladder
He's becoming a seer

Kurt's recovering
From a nasty fall
Now to keep peace
He can only call

Katy has shed
A ton of weight
She looks exquisite
Just downright great

Jack is the master
Of many sports
Soon he'll be dribbling
Around on the courts

Annie is learning
Gymnastics and Dancing
She also loves
To dress cute and fancy

Michael Bjorn
Is really a looker
But sometimes his language
Resembles a hooker's

Grandma, believe it or not
Is in school
She still reads and knits
And loves her O'Douls

Pop as always
Is looking down
He sends us his love
To us all he's still bound

Let's not forget
The reason we're here
We're all saying Thank You
For another good year

Amen

THANKSGIVING 2011

Grandma retired
Can you believe that?
Now she runs and she walks
For fear she'll get fat

Mike is sharing
His home once again
His rank as a father
Is a definite ten

Catrin as always
Puts forth the great feast
We all say our thank-you's
At the very, very least

Megan's a Co-Ed
To college she went
Here's hoping she doesn't
End up in a tent

Mikey is driving
A grown-up sight
He just needs to learn
Not to sneak out at night

Joey as always
Is smart as can be
But will he play baseball?
Guess we'll just wait and see

Kurt is always
A very good Dad
But, yes, there are times
When indeed he gets mad

Katy received
A very nice call
She did get the job
In spite of her fall

Jack is still
The all-around jock
In football he knows
How to hustle and block

Annie's a cheerleader
She really looks cute
She's right in style
From her hair to her boots

Michael is in Kindergarten
Getting taller each day
But he still needs to learn
There are things you can't say

Mary is travelling
All over the place
Her home displays
Her exquisite taste

Fred continues
To maintain the house
Except when he attacked
The weeds to de-louse

Helena is reading
Ahead of her time
She's a real darling girl
And she's learned not to whine

Margot displays
Her riotous curls
People stop and stare
At this beautiful girl

Martin is soon
To have a new child
It's hard to believe
That William won't go wild

Lauren is ever
The best little Mom
She's having Thanksgiving
At her brother Tom's

William's a tiger
The truest of boys
He'll soon have to learn
How to share all his toys

Pop as always is
Right on the scene
He sends down his blessings
To all of his team

Thank you for another
Bless-ed good year
Please keep us well
Give us nothing to fear

Amen

Vase and Candle at the Beach. (4/2004). Actylic and oil. 11 x 14 inches.

THANKSGIVING 2012

Today Is Thanksgiving
A bless-ed day
We've all come together
To laugh and to pray

Grandma's retired
And settling down
There's really no end
Of bus-i-ness to be found

Michael Anthony
Once again is our host
In giving to all
He is really the most

Catrin's at the oven
To keep us well fed
She even did pies this year
"Thank you, Thank you" Grandma said.

Megan is beautiful.
And does well in school
She now has a partner
Who is really a jewel

Mikey keeps everyone
On their toes
You just never know
What will be his next woe

Joey's a treasure
With many skills
He seems to excel
In whatever he wills

Kate has a new job
And it's going well
She's also the Queen of
Face Book do-tell

Kurt's a magician
In getting things done
His energy and strength
Make him number one

Jack's a jock
Who loves his sports
He's also excelling
In his school reports

Catherine Ann is
Pretty and keen
In basketball
She made the Travel Team

Meat-ball is tall
And ever so smart
He's even learning to say
"Excuse me" when he farts

Mary and crew are
In Puerto Rico
She's taking a break
And learning "un pocito"

Fred works hard and is a
Fabulous father
He gives the impression
That nothing's a bother

Helena just shed
Her two front teeth
She excels in most
Everything she seeks

Margot's still
A riot of curls
She's one of the
Prettiest of girls

Martin this year
Had a major promotion
If only he'd stop
Fearing a demotion

Lauren's as busy
As a bee
Her little ones keep her
Never free

William's a talker
And a very active child
At times he can
Even get a bit wild

Abby's an eater
She loves any food
She's one year old already
The littlest of our brood

Pop appears at all
Major gatherings
He dresses like a Cardinal
And still is fathering

Thank you from all
For a bless-ed year
May we always trust
And never fear

AMEN

THANKSGIVING 2013

It's time to be grateful
And say thank You so much
Once again we've been blessed
By Your heavenly touch

Grandma is faithful
About her three-mile walks
Even though her leg muscles
Sometimes balk

Michael outdid himself
In helping in Brick
His work ethic came through
As admirably strict

Catrin the lovely
Brings all her skills
To make sure that all of us
Have our Thanksgiving fills

Megan continues
On her path to success
And has a great partner
In her beau from out West

Mikey is industrious
What a worker!
On the side he also
Likes cigars and poker

Joey as always is
Full of talents
Does he never
Do bad things to balance?

Katy gave birth to
A beautiful boy
May he always bring
To all many joys

Kurt has been
Beyond busy this year
With problem after problem
He is always in gear

Jack looks great
And still plays many sports
He also has many friends
And impressive school reports

Annie's always in motion
Her energy sometimes soars
But more than anything
She's well-rounded and gets all good scores

Meat-Ball is still
A delightful child
But his gun-shooting does
Get a little wild

Matthew is lovely
And has filled the house
Sometimes he cries but
Sometimes is quiet as a mouse

Mary continues to travel
As her job demands
Her house is impressive
Grandma's a frequent fan

Fred is quite a Dad
He is thoroughly immersed
In all that it takes
To make him a fatherhood-first

Helena is now
Called Goldilocks
She's smart as a whip
Her school work really rocks

Margot, now called Curlylocks,
Is learning to read
This has been her dream
And she's starting to succeed

Martin's still
With Morgan Stanley
At home he tends to
His lovely family

Lauren continues
Busy as a bee
She has a new business
To add to her tree

William is fun
And full of life
His new interest is a "Bible"
And he preaches "no strife"

Abby turned two
And is a happy child
She eats well and sleeps well
And is rarely wild

Pop, we know,
Is with us today
He's always been here
And will always stay

May we humbly thank You
Once again
For the blessings that
You always send

Amen

THANKSGIVING 2014

It's Thanksgiving Day
And we all are here
Again we've been blessed
With another good year

Grandma hit a milestone
She's seventy-five
Still reading and knitting
And walking to thrive

Mike's filling his time
With a lot of big planning
First child to be married
A son-in-law soon landing

Catrin also has nary a minute
But somehow has planned our feast
She, too, had a big birthday
Not her favorite to say the least

Megan is a senior
College soon will be done
And upon graduation
A beautiful bride she will become

We welcome Jake
To the family feast
He's a brand new ensign
First rate to say the least

Mikey's a freshman
He's burning the lights
And both of his roommates
Are special delights

Joey's a cool dude
Smart and fit
As he drives his red Mazda
He surely makes hits

Katy's amazing
A Mommy of four
Incredibly busy
With work, home, and more

And speaking of busy
Kurt is certainly that
The Jack of all Trades
Raising kids, dogs and cats

Jack is a jock
Into football and LaCrosse
He has many good friends
And is usually the boss

Annie's a scholar
With consistent high grades
She's also an athlete
And her beauty brings raves

Michael in baseball
Broke a tied late score
He sure was a hero
To players and more

Matthew turned one
And is still a delight
But when Grandma appears
It gives him a fright

Mary continues
To travel and work
And still finds time
To share her culinary perks

Fred as always
Excels as a Dad
He supports and nurtures
When you're mad, bad, or sad

Helena has entered
An upper-class school
She ran for election
And she won – she's so cool!

Margot is reading
Taking piano, tennis and gym
She's a bundle of life
Her light never dims

Martin continues
His success in law
He golfs and runs
And races to malls

Lauren is saintly
With her super-active kids
She has her own business
Which helps provide a lid

William is growing
"I'm almost five!"
He's succeeding in school
And is oh so alive

Abby is having
A birthday today
She's just turned three
And loving ballet

Yes, Pop as always
Is with us today
He watches us all
In his own special way

Thank You once more
For a healthy year
If we stay close to You
We have nothing to fear

AMEN

THANKSGIVING 2015

It's time to say thank you
For all we've been given
Surely all of our blessings
Were showered from heaven

Grandma finally moved
From her big costly place
Her luxury digs
Put smiles on her face

Catrin and Mike
Were the hosts of the year
A beautiful wedding
That brought many a tear

Megan and Jake
Were a stunning pair
And now for a while
One's here and one's there

Mikey is now in
His sophomore year
He now rides the ultimate bike
But we all shall not fear

Joey our genius
Is surely on edge
Awaiting decisions
To whom will he pledge?

Katy and Kurt
Are an amazing pair
Managing the happy household
With hard work and care

Grandpa happily is here
For our thanksgiving feast
He brought his gaucamole
And treats for the beasts

Jack plays football
Undefeated so far
The tallest in his family
And soon will think "car"

Annie's a beauty
And a scholar to boot
She plays several sports
Her future holds loot

Michael is also a sportster
On undefeated teams
He's sporting new glasses
All looks better it seems

Matthew is beautiful
A happy delightful boy
His only problem
Lies in sharing his toys

Mary and Fred
Bought a baby grand
They also traverse
All over the land

Helena is a tall blonde beauty
With lots of skill layers
She loves to read
And excels as a piano player

Margot's losing her baby teeth
And looking for the tooth fairy
She, too, plays piano
And is admired for her curly hair

Lauren and Martin
Have embraced some new things
The sale of a townhouse
And a new business fling

William's at Willard
And loving it there
He's a very smart boy
And has toys everywhere

Abby is a beauty
Always in fancy attire
When she's pitted against William
She can light her own fire

Yes, Pop is always with us
Sending blesssings from above
He showers us with prayers and blessings
To remind us of his love

We are very grateful
For the time that pop was here
He endowed us all with gifts so great
That have guided us through our years

AMEN

THANKSGIVING 2016

Today is Thanksgiving
Our time to sing praise
To be grateful to God
For all our bles-sed days

Grandma is healthy
Not wealthy, but wise
Grateful to still be watching
Our beautiful family thrive

Catrin and Mike
Are hosting again
This day we all cherish
How generous they've been

Megan's in Seattle
Working very long hours
Her absence is always evident
She's our missing flower

Jake is mostly
Under the sea
Fulfilling a mission
That helps keep us free

Mikey is now
In his junior year
He's now even legal
To buy a beer!

Joe is a Freshman
At U. V. A.
He makes us so proud
Of his succeeding ways

Kate and Kurt
Continue to amaze
Their full family life
Is always ablaze

Jack broke his leg
In a Football bout
But played on for weeks
Before checking it out

Annie's a beauty
A scholar besides
She also plays Softball
And by all rules abides

Michael plays Baseball
And Basketball, too
And every now and then
He looks up from his lap view

Matthew's now three
No longer a wetter
He had his first "Time-Out"
And quickly learned better

Mary and Fred
Still travel for pleasure
Exposing the girls
To the world's wondrous treasures

Helena's an aspiring
Tennis Pro
And also puts on
A good keyboard show

Margot plays Softball
And also piano
Her infectious energy
Brings joy like Nirvana

Lauren and Martin
Continue to thrive
With Ty as their bedmate
Who's testing their drive

William's a wonder
No energy to spare
He continues to love Willard
And does very well there

Abby's a princess
A beautiful little jewel
And she still holds her own
In the daily sibling duals

We know that Pop
Is always here
He savors our blessings
And calms our fears

We thank our Heavenly Father
For Pop's time in our lives
And for the many wonderful things
That he taught us to prize

Amen

THANKSGIVING 2017

Twenty seventeen
A bles-sed year
We thank you God
From all of us here

Mom wrote a book
Of family and God
And went on a cruise
To foreign sod

Michael as always
Stands strong on his feet
It often seems
There's no need he can't meet

Catrin took a job
At a popular store
She continues to feast us
Offering more and more

Megan's a Mommy
Asa's his name
We all were so happy
On the day that he came

Jake is off-shore
Serving our land
He sees his new family
As much as he can

Mikey is studying
By day and by night
And both of his roommates
Are special delights

Joey still ranks
In school where he rocks
An honor-roll student
With long flowing locks

Katy and Kurt
Are amazing parents
So much to keep up with
So no one goes errant

Jack is a big guy
Now six foot one
Accepted already
In two college runs

Annie lettered
This year as a freshman
What an accomplishment
An outstanding exception

Michael loves baseball
His favorite sport
But he's glued to his lap-top
And they need to part

Matthew is a dear one
A bright little boy
To make him happy
Just bring a new toy

Mary and Fred
Run a really tight ship
They excel at parenting
As they crack the whip

Helena has braces
And many talents she wields
She's an impressive young lady
Who excels in many fields

Margot is delightful
Our curly-locks doll
She plays the piano
And excels at playing ball

Lauren and Martin
Both work to say the least
They have a new Nanny
Who helps keep the peace

William's a sportster
He slugs left-handed
He's happy in school
And his talk is incessant

Abby's a princess
She dresses so chic-ly
She's also a dancer
And speaks rather meekly

Our Dad is with us
In his heavenly way
We wish he were with us
On this special day

We thank our dear Lord
For Dad's time on earth
And are grateful to him
For sharing his worth

AMEN

THANKSGIVING 2018

Christmas is nearing
As we give You our thanks
The year has been blessed
With joy and sorrow in our ranks

Grandma is still walking
And still baking pies
She also had surgery
To correct her eyes

Michael remains
A successful Dude
We missed him this Thanksgiving
And his family and his food

Catrin and Mike are
Flying the skies
Cherishing little Asa
Until they say their goodbyes

Catrin is of course
A perfect grandmother
Tending to her extended family
And serving any others

Megan is doing
A lot of travelling
She also works
And still isn't unravelling

Jake is scouting
Graduate schools
And it won't be long
Before he leaves military rules

Asa fills the hearts
Of our total clan
And it looks like he'll grow
To be a tall husky man

Mikey is nearing
The end of college
This success is indeed
Worthy to acknowledge

Joe managed two jobs while schooling
And lived for four months in mold and murk
He also would seem to like dogs
More than people or other work

Katy had an accident
That ended her work
And now is a house Mom
And excelling in worth

Kurt continues to be
A man of all trades
He cooks and drives
And endures all the charades

Jack's in college
And it's going great
Who would have guessed
That he'd go so straight

Annie's still a scholar
With very high scores
She also plays softball
And never seems bored

Michael has become
A successful pitcher
And his new school has made
His grades ever richer

Matthew remains
A complete delight
He keeps the house alive
From morning to night

Mary continues
Her successful career
And manages somehow
To produce incredible meals

Fred is the house Dad
From morning to night
Between coaching, work, and daughters
He balances till all is right

Helena gave us a scare
With a sickness that really ruled
But all is well now
With piano, tennis, and school

Margot is truly
A pretty young girl
She does her own hair now
And somehow manages those curls

Martin remains
With Morgan Stanley
He's thinking about
A big new shanty

Lauren had a
Sadness this year
But she has a new job
Which keeps her more near

Will's into baseball
Including being a pitcher
He does well in school, too
Which makes his life even richer

Abby's a dancer
And a sweet young girl
She also is quite a reader
As each book she unfurls

Our love to Pop
And to Pop-Pop, too
May God give blessings and love
To both of you

We know Dad is watching
And sending his love
We're happy to share you
From up above

AMEN

THANKSGIVING 2019

Today is Thanksgiving
Our year has been good
We send You our gratitude
As well we should.

Mom turned eighty
A hefty age
Working to stay healthy
To turn the next page.

Our numbers are stable
We're still twenty-two
We feel very blessed
To savor our crew.

Mike is working on
Staying in shape
We pray he's successful
And no rules does he break.

Catrin remains
The loveliest one
Wherever she goes
She brings out the sun.

Mikey was feted
At a graduation party
We all had such fun
And no one was too rowdy.

Joe remains
Our genius child
Now all are wondering
What will be his next trial.

Megan is managing
To do it all
Working and Mommying
And holding up the walls.

Jake has become
A graduate student
His school choice has definitely been
More than prudent.

Asa the sweetheart
Is a beautiful boy
We all are in love with
How cute and how coy.

Katy is recovering
From a major procedure
Hopefully this will end
Her long-standing seizure.

Kurt remains
The task-master king
Among the many household chores
He can and will do anything.

Jack is proving to be
Quite the scholar
Mom and Dad are proud
Of their studious feller.

Annie was nominated
For Homecoming Queen
Her beauty is dazzling
She's such a dream.

Michael continues at the
Oratory School
His baseball skills
Continue to rule.

Matthew turned six
A lively, lovely boy
He has many friends
And many, many toys.

Mary is now a partner
In a new legal job
She works from home now
Amidst the mob.

Fred bought a Deli
The shock of all shocks
Now he and David
Are raising up the stocks.

Helena's semi-military
In her new prep school
She continues to grow
And to live up to her rules.

Margot is becoming
A masterful cook
And continues to excel
In her softball nook.

Martin continues to
Pull in success
He worries and frets
And still does the best.

Lauren is a trainer
A new career
She's close to home
So everyone's near.

Will is a good student
There's nothing he will miss
And an absolute genius
As a baseball whiz.

Abby is active and
Playing basketball
She's pretty and chic
And dances off the walls.

We know that Pop
Is watching closely
To assure that we all
Are progressing nicely.

God bless him
In his home in the skies
Just sorry that he has
To miss all the pies.

Please treat him as
Your special angel
To help keep us safe
And free from danger.

AMEN

Dr. Frank Stringfellow, scientist, author, poet, painter, and storyteller, was born in Northampton County on the eastern shore of Virginia on October 27, 1940. He received his early schooling in the public schools there (Atlantic High School, now Arcadia). Surrounded by creative, talented, and well-educated family members, Frank absorbed a love of nature, his fellow man, and storytelling that knew no bounds. His family's early roots and extensive web of kin filled him with a rich repertoire of life's stories.

Frank graduated from St. Louis University with a degree in biology in 1962. In 1964, he earned a Master of Arts degree in biology from Drake University. From there, he was offered an instructorship at the University of South Carolina where he completed his Ph.D. in biology in 1967. He obtained advanced training in pathology through the Veterans Administration and studied further in Pathology at the Armed Forces Institute of Pathology.

Frank won a position as a research scientist at the world renowned Lab, the Animal Parasitology Institute, United States Department of Agriculture, Beltsville, Maryland. He worked for over thirty-one years as a research scientist and authored over forty scientific publications, most numerously in *The Journal of Parasitology*.

Frank is now retired and enjoys his family, especially his three young granddaughters. He continues a lifelong passion for sharing his love of nature.

He received the Maryland Governor's Award for Leadership in Aging for Art in 2011.

www.ingramcontent.com/pod-product-compliance
Lightning Source LLC
Chambersburg PA
CBHW060340080526

44584CB00013B/847